WHO REALLY DISCOVERED
AMERICA?

WHO REALLY DISCOVERED AMERICA?

by STEPHEN KRENSKY

illustrated by STEVE SULLIVAN

HASTINGS HOUSE BOOK PUBLISHERS
New York

This edition is published in 1991 by Hastings House by arrangement with Scholastic, Inc. Text copyright © 1987 by Stephen Krensky. Illustrations copyright © 1987 by Scholastic Books Inc.

For information regarding permission, write to Scholastic, Inc., 730 Broadway, New York, New York 10003.

ISBN: 0-8038-9306-X

Hastings House
Book Publishers
Mamaroneck, New York 10543

Distributed to the trade by Publishers Group West
Emeryville, California 94608

Printed in the U.S.A.

10 9 8 7 6 5 4 3 2 1

For my grandparents,
who discovered America, too.

—*S.K.*

INTRODUCTION

Christopher Columbus has always gotten most of the credit for discovering America. He got the fame and he got the holiday. If things had gone a little differently, America might have been named for him, too. Columbus, though, was not the first to discover America. How could he be? After all, there were people here to greet him when he arrived. Columbus called them Indians because he thought he had reached islands near India. He was wrong about that, but the name Indian *stuck to the natives anyway.*

Although these Indians lived in America, they had not discovered it, either. They had simply been born there. So had their parents and grandparents. The Indians did not know when their ancestors had first arrived in America. Since records were not kept, they did not know when anyone had arrived. America was a big place. Had just one people settled there at one time or many peoples at different times? And where had they come from? What had brought them to America? What did they find when they arrived? These questions are all part of the mystery of who really discovered America.

THE FIRST AMERICANS

BEFORE ANYONE COULD discover America, there first had to be an America to discover. The earth is over four billion years old. For most of that time—over millions of years—there was no land at all. The ocean covered everything. Then the seas fell, the mountains rose, and the land appeared. This land was all one piece, though. There were not yet any separate continents. Africa and South America fit together like pieces in a jigsaw puzzle. Australia was just a big bump at the bottom of Asia.

Two hundred million years ago the land began to break apart. The future continents began to shift. North America went one way, Europe and Asia went another. Africa tugged down, creating the Mediterranean sea above it. South America pulled free of Africa, but just barely held on to North America. (See illustration, p. 10.) Australia and Antarctica broke off on their own.

The continents settled into their present places about 65 million years ago, about the same time as the dinosaurs disappeared.

Asia

North America

Europe

South America

Africa

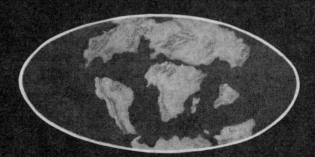

Many earth scientists believe that 200 million years ago there was one great land mass and one huge ocean on the earth. As time passed, the land broke apart creating the continents and oceans we know today.

Dinosaurs had ruled the earth for 130 million years. Now mammals had their turn. Mastodons and mammoths—bigger than elephants—roamed the countryside. Saber-toothed tigers prowled the forests. Horses, camels, and dogs tried to keep out of their way.

These animals had America to themselves for over 64 million years. Near the end of that time, a million years ago, the Ice Age began. Temperatures dropped. Great sheets of ice called *glaciers* crept south from the North Pole. Some of these glaciers were thousands of feet thick. Whole forests disappeared under them; the trees snapped off like twigs. Deep valleys were cut in the earth. Huge rocks were moved hundreds of miles.

All that ice used up a lot of water. This water had once run down rivers and streams, helping to fill the ocean. Now it was freezing over much of the land. As less water poured into the ocean, the sea level dropped. It was not until thousands of years later, when the ice melted, that the water returned to the sea, and the oceans rose again.

The glaciers came south four times. Each time, the shallow sea bottom between Siberia and Alaska (now known as the Bering Strait) was completely uncovered. The exposed ocean floor became a land bridge linking Asia and North America. This was no small passageway. It was a swampy plain a thousand miles wide.

For a long time nobody was around to use the land bridge between the two continents. The time of the first crossing is not yet known for sure, but it may have taken place as long as 40,000 years ago. The first people to cross were simply follow-

ing herds of wild game. When the herds wandered into America, these people followed after them.

These people were the first Americans. (As far as we know, no people actually evolved in America. The first ones here had to come from somewhere else.) They did not know that they had discovered America. In those days people didn't worry about discovering places. They worried about food and shelter. They were able to make fires, and they hunted animals with spears, eating the meat and using the hides for clothing.

For thousands of years many different peoples used the land bridge. Everyone (except the Eskimos) gradually traveled south. People stayed in one place for a month or a year. Time didn't matter. When the food was gone, they moved on. There was no reason to hurry, though, and nobody did. People finally reached the southern tip of South America about 10,000 years ago.

Along the way the early Americans hunted down huge numbers of mastodons, bison, and horses. Sometimes they stampeded a whole herd over a cliff — a quick and easy method that left more dead animals than the hunters could use.

Changes in the weather, though, greatly affected these early settlers. The last Ice Age ended about 10,000 years ago. In the next 3,000 years temperatures rose. The land bridge between Asia and North America was again covered by water. Much of

Early settlers from the continent of Asia may have hunted giant mastodon in prehistoric America.

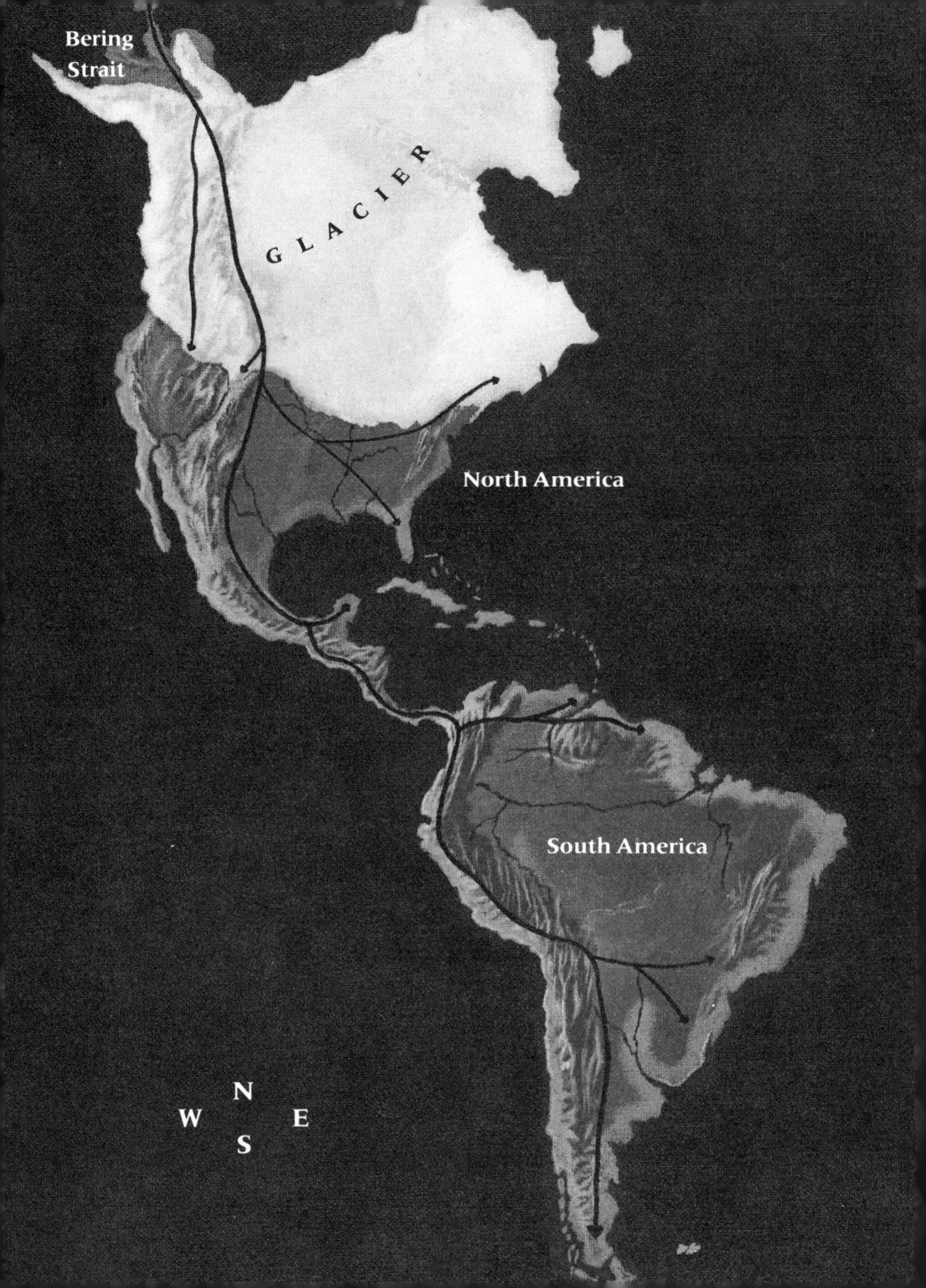

Bering Strait
GLACIER
North America
South America
N
W
E
S

the grazing land dried out. Without the long grasses to eat, the mammoths and mastodons could not survive. The new Americans continued to hunt them, though, until they were all gone.

As the big animals disappeared, people began hunting smaller animals. This was much harder than hunting big animals. Smaller animals did not travel in herds. To catch them, people had to become more inventive. Inland hunters built snares to capture rabbits or squirrels. Coastal hunters developed a spear to skewer fish.

Smaller animals also influenced the new Americans' travel habits. Big animals had roamed widely. So the hunters who followed them roamed widely, too. Small animals stayed longer in one place. Since they didn't move, the hunters didn't move, either. This gave people more time to explore their land. If the soil was rich, they even had time to plant crops. If they raised grain, they began grinding it with stones to make flour. Making flour led to making bread. Once people had bread and vegetables, they didn't have to hunt so much.

One person could now grow more food than he alone could eat. Just a few farmers could feed many other people. This gave the others time to think about new ideas — like building better homes and developing trade with other communities. Soon they weren't just thinking anymore, they were actually building and trading.

The first Americans probably traveled from Asia to Alaska on foot across what is now the Bering Strait. Over thousands of years they made their way south, settling throughout North and South America.

15

None of these people thought of America as special, or as separate from the Asia their ancestors had come from. America was home, and they made the most of it. Over the next few thousand years, their descendants would create three great American civilizations — the Incas, the Maya, and the Aztecs. These cultures remain a lasting tribute to the first discoverers of America.

VISITORS FROM THE
PACIFIC

THE FIRST DISCOVERY of America was the only one that came by land. Later discoveries were made by sea because the land bridge between Siberia and Alaska was gone. The ocean had covered it up again.

The first sea travelers also came from Asia, but their route is not easy to follow. The ocean hides its trails well. There is evidence, though, that some people sailed east to America even if they didn't do it on purpose.

Along the coast of Ecuador in South America archaeologists have investigated the sites of villages that are 5,000 years old. (The area itself may have been settled 15,000 years ago.) In many ways these villages were like hundreds of others along the South American coast. The people caught fish from the sea and

17

gathered food from the countryside. The archaeologists found both fishing hooks and woven baskets among the village remains. They also found something else, something that seemed out of place—broken pieces of pottery.

The pottery was a surprise. These fisherfolk had no heritage of making pots. And these were not crude first attempts. They were graceful and detailed. How could the villagers have made them?

Maybe the villagers hadn't made the pots themselves. If they hadn't, who had? Nobody nearby made such pots. Could it have been someone from far away? Other pottery-making cultures of the same period were examined and compared. Strangely, the Ecuador pots most closely resembled pots of the Jomon people of Japan. The Jomon people were also fisherfolk, but they were skilled potters as well. Could Japanese pots have made their way across the Pacific ocean?

Some investigators think so. They guess that a storm blew a boatload of Jomon fishermen out to sea. There, ocean currents carried them northward to Alaska, then south along the west coast of the Americas (see map, pages 32-33). Once the Jomon fishermen reached Ecuador, they could have taught pottery-making to the natives or just made the pottery there themselves.

But did this happen? Maybe yes and maybe no. The Jomon visit makes a good story, but it raises some interesting questions,

The Jomon people of ancient Japan were skilled fishermen and excellent potters. There is evidence to suggest that they may have accidentally crossed the Pacific Ocean bringing their knowledge of pottery-making to Ecuador.

too. If Japanese fishermen were carried by currents to North America, why did they then travel all the way south to Ecuador? Why didn't they stop in Canada or California or a hundred other places? Why risk their lives traveling thousands of extra miles in a little fishing boat? Nobody has answers for these questions yet. Until answers are found, the mystery of the pots will remain a mystery.

Small fishing boats, however, were not the only vessels that could be carried to America. Large ships could also be caught by storms and currents. By 250 B.C. great ships from India and China were sailing through southeast Asian waters. These ships traded in many goods including gold, silver, and spices. They were well stocked with food and water, and capable of long voyages.

Would any of these ships have deliberately sailed eastward? Well, there was a Chinese legend about certain islands that supposedly existed in the Eastern sea (the Pacific ocean). These were magical places where the animals were completely white, and the palaces were made of gold and silver. For centuries Chinese sea captains had searched for these islands. They had not found even one.

In 219 B.C. the explorer Hsu Fu asked the Chinese emperor for permission to search for the islands. The emperor agreed, but he grumbled about the cost of the expedition. Hsu Fu was

Hsu Fu, a Chinese sea captain, left China around 200 B.C. with 3,000 young men and women on a voyage of discovery. They never returned. Their ship was large and strong enough to have made the trip across the Pacific, but no evidence of their arrival in America has yet been found.

not leaving with a single ship. He was leading a great fleet with many supplies and 3,000 men and women.

Hsu Fu left with the emperor's high hopes. Those hopes were not high for long. The emperor expected the voyage to be long, but he also expected Hsu Fu to return. In this he was disappointed. Hsu Fu never came back. Neither did any of the ships or the 3,000 young men and women.

Where did they go? Many historians believe they settled in Japan (which is, after all, an island east of China). It's possible, of course, that Hsu Fu and his great fleet reached America. Yet no sign of this visit has been found so far. If 3,000 Chinese people had landed in America over 2,000 years ago, they would have built a city or perhaps an empire. Even if their buildings were later destroyed, ruins would be left. If such ruins are ever discovered, there will be little doubt about who made them.

In the following centuries Chinese and Indian ships continued to trade in the Southwest Pacific and Indian oceans. They reached the islands of Java and Sumatra, sea journeys of many hundreds of miles. But none of them ever stumbled across America, at least not officially. The Chinese kept careful records of where their ships went. As of A.D. 285 they still reported that no one they knew had crossed the Eastern Sea.

Of course a Chinese or Indian ship could have reached America by accident. If it never returned, no one at home would learn of the discovery. The ship would only be remembered as having been lost at sea.

There are several cultural signs that some Asian ships must have made the trip. The strongest links are in art and architec-

The art of Mayan civilization in America bears a striking resemblance to that found in the early art of India. The bloom of the lotus flower was a common design motif in both civilizations.

ture. One recurring symbol in the art of India also appears in the Mayan art of South America. It is the lotus flower. Did these two great cultures single out this flower by chance? What about the decorative details on buildings? The stylized people and animals are often very similar. There are ancient Mexican pots that look much like ancient Chinese pots. They both have lids with rings at the top or handles shaped like birds.

Games and toys share some features, too. The Hindu game of pachisi has been played in India for thousands of years. The Mexican game of Patolli (which the Aztecs were playing when the Spaniards arrived in the 1500's) has a similar board and pieces. The rules also have much in common. And some ancient toys that were dug up in Mexico have features similar to ancient Asian designs. The wheels on these toys have drawn special attention. They are the only wheels ever found in America that were made before the time of Columbus. The ancient American civilizations had no horses, mules, or donkeys to pull things around. (These animals were later imported from Europe.) Therefore, they apparently had no reason to invent the wheel for themselves. So who thought up the toy wheels? Were they made by Chinese sailors who had sailed into a Mexican port? Or did they wash ashore from a Chinese shipwreck at sea?

The lotus flower, architectural designs, pottery styles, games, and toys all point to some ancient contact between America and the cultures of China or India. The links probably would be stronger if a colony of Chinese or Indians had actually settled in America. Perhaps Chinese or Indian objects survived the long sea voyage while the sailors themselves did not. Or maybe the native Americans did not welcome the strange-looking visitors arriving out of their sunset. The Chinese or

Indian sailors may simply have been killed, and the goods they carried copied later. One thing seems certain. Whatever contact there was, it was unplanned and short-lived.

One other Asian group, the Polynesians, had the chance to discover America by sea. These people were scattered over many islands in the South Pacific. They traveled in large canoes that could hold forty or fifty passengers. Their double canoes, joined by two bars and a small platform, could hold many more. The Polynesians hopscotched around the Pacific islands, making known voyages of as long as 1,800 miles. It is only 2,000 miles from Hawaii to the northwest American coast.

But did contact take place? Unlike the Chinese or Indians, the Polynesians seem to have left nothing of their own in America. No Polynesian art or games or toys have been found mixed in with ancient American remains. So what proof of their visits exists?

The proof lies with the humble sweet potato. The sweet potato is known to have first appeared only in America. Yet when European explorers reached the Pacific islands of Polynesia in the 1700's, they found sweet potatoes growing there — and not just a few sweet potatoes, either. So many sweet potatoes were growing on so many islands that it was clear that sweet potatoes had been cultivated there for hundreds of years.

How did they get there? It is unlikely that early Americans made a one-way voyage to Polynesia with sweet potatoes on board. They were not widely known for taking ocean voyages.

And sweet potatoes did not make the trip by themselves. They could not float across the Pacific (the way coconuts could). They also had to be deliberately planted.

So although the Japanese, Chinese, and Indian visitors may have come to America and stayed, some Polynesians who came here apparently went home again. Americans may have gained little from the Polynesian visits, but at least the Polynesians got sweet potatoes for having made the trip.

EARLY
ATLANTIC CROSSINGS

THERE ARE MANY stories of European explorers crossing the Atlantic before Columbus. Most of them were invented by Europeans who came here after Columbus. These people could not believe that American civilizations as advanced as the Aztecs had developed without their help. Someone from a Western civilization, they thought, must have reached America earlier and given the New World a helping hand.

Clearly some stories of ships crossing the Atlantic are more likely than others. Connections were once drawn between the ancient Egyptians and the Maya of Central America largely because both cultures built pyramids. But the pyramids are very different. The Egyptian pyramids were built as burial tombs. The Mayan ones had no usable space on the inside. The Egyptian pyramids rose to a point. Their outsides were not designed to be used. The Mayan pyramids often included steps that could be climbed. Their tops were also cut off, creating a usable space

The Phoenicians were the merchant seamen of the ancient western world. They traded throughout the Mediterranean and as far north as Britain.

for many purposes. Had the two kinds of pyramids come from a single culture, they wouldn't have been as different as that.

Besides, the Egyptians were not a seagoing people. When they had serious sailing to do, they hired the Phoenicians to do it. The Phoenicians were a nation of merchants and traders that settled on the eastern coast of the Mediterranean about 5,000 years ago. Hemmed in by Egyptian, Assyrian, and later Babylonian empires, the Phoenicians never controlled a lot of land. They built their empire on the sea. They founded Carthage in

North Africa in the eighth century B.C. and established a port at the site of the present city of Cadiz, Spain, a hundred years later. By 450 B.C. they had even sailed to England to trade for tin.

Their greatest voyage, though, was reported by the ancient Greek historian, Herodotus. In the sixth century B.C. Phoenicians working for Egyptian Pharaoh Necho set sail southward along the African coast. Their ships were large row galleys, eighty to one hundred feet long. Each ship used one square sail. When the wind failed, the sailors manned oars that stuck out from the sides of the ship like the legs of a giant insect.

The Phoenicians were planning to sail all around Africa. They did not expect it to be a long trip because they didn't think Africa was very big. As the voyage continued, they learned otherwise. Since there had been little space for food on the crowded ships, the crew now regularly went ashore and planted crops. Then they waited several months for the crops to grow. Naturally this slowed their progress. In the end, the trip took three years.

Various tales have given the Phoenicians credit for going everywhere from Brazil to New Hampshire. These tales usually rest on the evidence of rocks inscribed with messages the Phoenicians left behind. In these cases people have mistaken ordinary cracks in the rocks for Phoenician letters, which do look a lot like rock cracks.

The Phoenicians, however, could have reached America. The Atlantic Ocean is less than 2,000 miles wide between the western bulge of Africa and the eastern bulge of South America. A current there also runs westward from Africa. A Phoenician ship sailing around Africa could be blown off course and then sail across to Brazil.

Did the Phoenicians do this? Well, in 1872 a stone was supposedly found in Brazil covered with Phoenician writing. It told of a ship that had been separated in a storm from a fleet going around Africa from Egypt. The storm had blown the ship across the sea to this new land.

Was this proof of a Phoenician visit? The facts fit nicely with the Herodotus story. The message even mentioned the Egyptian pharaoh Necho. And if a Phoenician ship had crossed the Atlantic, Brazil was certainly the most likely landing place.

Experts were eager to examine the stone further. Unfortunately, this was not possible — the stone had disappeared. All that remained was a copy of the message it contained. Scholars have argued about the message ever since. Some think it was authentic. Others think it was phony — a hodgepodge of grammar and words from different periods. The fact that the stone vanished is odd. It is also suspicious. Without examining the stone itself, nobody can truly know if it was authentic or not.

The Phoenicians may not have crossed the Atlantic in ancient times, but they were not alone. The great European conquerors of the next 1,500 years — Alexander the Great, Julius Caesar, Charlemagne—did most of their conquering by land. The reason lay partly with geography. They had plenty of countries to conquer without bothering to cross the ocean looking for more.

To push farther out into dangerous and unknown oceans,

SIBERIA

ALASKA

Prehistoric Man

ASIA

THE
BERING STRAIT

Jomon Voyage?

N O
AM

JAPAN

POLYNESIA

Polynesian Voya

GREENLAND

ICELAND

NORWAY

The Vikings

ENGLAND

John Cabot

A

SPAIN

PHOENICIA

Christopher Columbus

AFRICA

Phoenicians?

SOUTH
AMERICA

33

people needed a very good reason. The Egyptians, Greeks, and Romans never had one. Though they fought a few great sea battles, they fought them close to European shores. The focus of their conquests was always on land.

Seventh-century Vikings, on the other hand, often traveled by sea. They were a people living in Scandinavia — Norway Sweden, and Denmark — and their life was not easy. The winters were bitter cold. The summers were very short. Farming was difficult because the land was frozen over half the year. As the population grew, it was harder for everyone to get enough to eat.

In Scandinavia the Vikings had only one another to fight for land and food. They didn't want to do that. The sea was the quickest route to finding someone else to bother. So around A.D. 800 the Vikings sailed off in search of food, treasure, and new lands. They took their long open ships east toward Russia, west to England, and south to France. They even explored to the north — at least during the summer (see map, page 38).

To the northwest was Iceland, an island originally settled by Irish monks. The Vikings arrived about A.D. 870 and soon put themselves in charge. Some settlers came to Iceland for land or adventure. Others were sent there for causing trouble at home. Eric the Red was one of the troublemakers. He was banished from Norway for killing a neighbor in a fight.

In Iceland Eric got into another fight. Nobody was killed, but still Eric was banished from Iceland for three years. Some

In search of new land and high adventure, the Vikings learned to sail the treacherous waters of the North Atlantic.

people might have worried about running out of places to go. Not Eric. He got himself a ship and crew to explore further westward. He set sail in A.D. 982.

Three years later he returned to Iceland with tales of Greenland, as he called it. This was a huge country where icy mountains sat within sight of the ocean. The land wasn't really very green, but Eric thought a good name would encourage more people to return with him. And he was right. The next year he led twenty-five ships back across several hundred miles of open sea to Greenland. The ships were battered by storms, though. Only fourteen actually arrived.

Among the 400 colonists was a man named Herjulf. His son, Bjarni Herjulfson, lived in Norway and visited him every summer in Iceland. When Bjarni arrived for his usual visit in the summer of A.D. 986, though, he learned that his father had moved to Greenland.

Bjarni decided to follow his father. Nobody on his ship had ever been to Greenland, but that didn't stop him. He just sailed off in what seemed to him like the right direction. Three days later the ship was hemmed in by fog and drifted off course. When the fog cleared, the crew saw land. But this land was flat and wooded. Did Greenland have so many trees? Where were the icy mountains they had heard about?

Bjarni had just discovered a piece of North America, but he wasn't very curious about it. He was looking for Greenland, after all, which he thought must be further north. So he ordered his crew to sail northward. Twice more they saw land. Both times Bjarni's crew wanted to go ashore for food and water.

Bjarni would not let them. He may have thought it was too dangerous. Or he may have been impatient to see his father.

After nine days Bjarni sighted land fitting Greenland's description. Here he finally went ashore. This, in fact, was Greenland, and he found his father living close by. Bjarni never returned to America. He settled down in Greenland with his father and lived happily ever after.

Some people were surprised that Bjarni had not stopped to explore the strange new lands. Still, fourteen years passed before someone went back to find them. That someone was Leif Ericson, Eric the Red's son. He bought Bjarni's ship and hired thirty-five men to take on the expedition.

His ship retraced Bjarni's course in reverse order (see map, page 38). Traveling south, Leif first saw a barren land that he called Helluland (probably Baffin Island). Another sighting, which was level and wooded, Leif called Markland (probably Labrador). Two days later he saw land again. This was the land Bjarni had sighted first. Leif and his crew went ashore there and built themselves a house.

When spring came, Leif loaded his ship with grapes and timber. Then he sailed home to Greenland. The grapes were big news. The Vikings could make wine from grapes, and they liked to drink wine. In honor of the grapes, Leif named this land Vinland.

For many years historians questioned whether this voyage had ever been made. Leif's story was passed by word of mouth for two hundred years before it was ever written down. The Vikings had a tradition of telling heroic sagas, but how many of

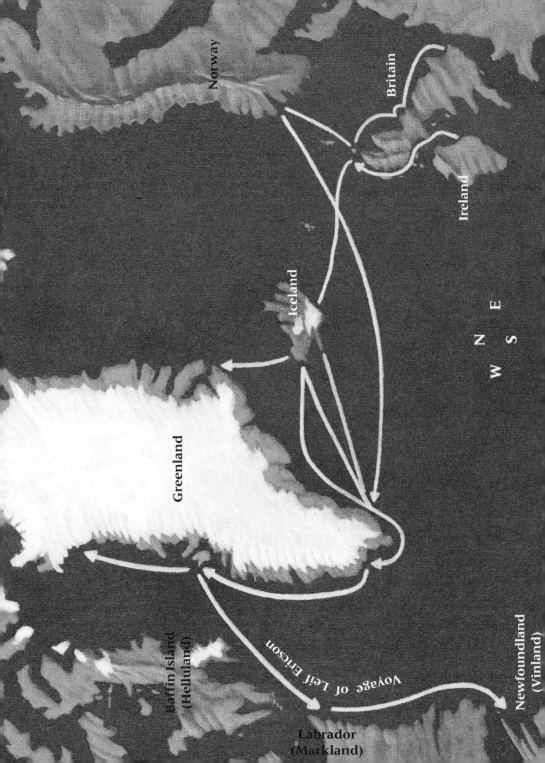

them were simply made-up legends? If Leif Ericson had gone ashore in America, where were the remains of his settlement? The grapes in the story pointed the way south because grapes do not grow north of New England. Had Leif reached Cape Cod? Some people even speculated that he went ashore off Chesapeake Bay in Maryland. But the distances involved were too great for the time mentioned in the Viking tales. This led the search northward again. The remains of Leif's settlement were finally found at L'Anse aux Meadows in northern New-foundland, the large island just off the eastern coast of Canada (see map, page 38).

So how can the grapes be explained? Maybe the Vikings really found cranberries (which can grow much farther north than grapes). The cranberries may have become grapes as the Vinland tales were retold and exaggerated over time. Or Leif may have stretched the truth himself to begin with. After all, if his father Eric could call Greenland green, Leif could certainly call cranberries grapes.

Members of Leif's family attempted four later trips to Vin-land. None ended as happily as his. Although later Viking trips to Vinland may have been made, no permanent colonies were started. The problem lay with the Greenland settlement, the jumping-off place for any American voyages. If the Greenlanders had thrived, more voyages would have been made. Greenland, though, became dependent on Norway for many supplies, and

The Vikings sailed throughout the North Atlantic, establishing colonies in Britain, Iceland, and Greenland. Leif Ericson probably explored as far south as Newfoundland in northeastern Canada.

in the next two hundred years, the fortunes of Norway declined. Fewer and fewer Norwegian ships sailed to Greenland for trade. As the Greenlanders struggled for survival, any thoughts of Vinland were pushed aside. The last mention of Vinland in Viking records came in 1347. The Greenland settlement itself, which had supported a thousand people in Leif Ericson's time, died out around 1500.

Much of what we know about the Vikings is based on the sagas that tell of the voyages of Leif Ericson.

Ancient square sail rigging

Improved lateen sails

Ocean going "galleons" in the time of Columbus combined square and lateen sails for speed and stability.

EAST BY WEST

IN THE CENTURIES after the Viking discovery of Vinland, the European world changed. The hundreds of feudal lords ruling their independent estates banded together under a smaller number of kings and queens. As governments organized, the need for communication between distant points grew. Kings and queens needed to know what was happening in all parts of their kingdoms. So better roads were built. As travel became safer, trade grew.

There always had been people who liked to explore the seas. Unfortunately exploring was expensive. There were ships to buy and sailors to hire. Few explorers were rich. They had to be sponsored by wealthy merchants or nobles. Even kings and queens were not interested in exploring for its own sake. But as traders began to look for new markets, they took to the seas.

*Advances in ship and sail design permitted faster
and safer travel on the high seas.*

Advances in ship design further improved sea travel. In the Middle Ages ships had one mast and a square sail made of wool. The sails were heavy and awkward, and got worse when they were wet. Around the year 1200 sails started to be made from flax or canvas. They were lighter and shed water more easily. Sails were also changing shape. Lateen sails, which were triangular, came into use. They caught the wind from either side much better than square sails. Soon ships had many kinds of sails and more than one mast to hold them.

Where were these new and improved ships going? If they sailed across the ocean, would they fall off the edge of the earth? Illiterate peasants may have thought so, but knowledgeable fifteenth-century sailors knew the earth was round. (The ancient Greeks had proven this more than 1,700 years earlier.)

Seafaring men, though, had other superstitions to worry about. Portuguese sailors were afraid to head south around the African coast. They believed that near the equator there were boiling seas where huge sea serpents ruled the waves. What ship could face these obstacles and survive?

The sailors had heard these stories from the Moors of North Africa. The Moors had invented the stories to discourage the Portuguese from exploring. For many years this strategy worked. The closer Portuguese ships got to the equator, the more terrified the ship crews became. They always forced their captains to turn back.

Finally in 1434 the Portuguese captain Gil Eanes pushed his ship into the dreaded waters. Did he find boiling seas or sea serpents waiting for him? No. All he found was more ocean.

Africa was not the only attraction for these explorers. They were also looking for a sea route to the Orient. Pressure to find one had been building since Bubonic Plague had struck Europe in 1347. The Black Death, so named because of the dark bruises that appeared on the body, killed half the population in Europe within twenty years. Trade within Europe virtually stopped. Overland trade with the Orient, by which silk, spices, and other Asian goods came to Europe, also suffered greatly. Caravans that carried European goods were no longer so welcome in Asia. Villagers were nervous. Who knew which caravan was carrying another outbreak of sickness?

It took Europe almost a hundred years to recover from the Plague. Then in 1453 the Turks defeated European armies to capture Constantinople. That city, sitting between the Black and Aegean seas, was the focus of the East-West land trade. Now the Turks closed it off from Europe.

Rich Europeans, however, had grown too accustomed to silk and spices to give them up. So the explorers went to sea looking for another route to the Orient. The Portuguese led the way. They had already explored some of the African coast and discovered the Azores in the Atlantic. Unfortunately they could not afford to keep exploring in so many directions at once. They had to make a choice. Should they concentrate their attention in the Atlantic or continue exploring south around Africa? In 1474 the king of Portugal, Alfonso V, chose Africa.

Two years later a young sailor was on a ship traveling from Genoa, Italy, to England. The French, who were almost always at war with the English, attacked the ship. The ship sank off the

European trade with the Orient depended on caravans that traveled the great land routes from Asia. But the routes were abandoned when the fear of Black Death gripped all Europe. Caravans were suspected of carrying the sickness and the search began for a sea route to Asia.

Hangchow

Silk

CHINA

INDIA

Kabul

Tashkent

Spices

PERSIA

ARABIA

Mecca

Moscow

Constantinople

Perfume

BRITAIN

EUROPE

Portuguese coast. The young man, though, whose name was Christopher Columbus, made it safely to shore.

Columbus was twenty-five years old, and he had already been to sea for six years. He was not lucky that his ship sank, but he was lucky that his brother, Bartholomew, was a map-maker in nearby Lisbon. Columbus soon went into his business with him.

In Lisbon Columbus studied mathematics and astronomy so that he could be a navigator. In 1477 he sailed north on a ship bound for Ireland, England, and Iceland. In the northern ports there was some talk of lands across the ocean, but it was still only talk.

During the next thirteen years Columbus got married, lived in the Azores (and learned much about the Atlantic), and tried to get some European monarch to sponsor his trip of discovery. Columbus was convinced he could sail west to China and Japan. The Portuguese, who were concentrating on Africa, were not interested. Neither were the English. But Columbus did not give up. He believed he was destined for greatness.

The Spanish had already turned Columbus down once. He was about to try the French king when Ferdinand and Isabella, the rulers of Spain, changed their minds. They agreed to supply Columbus with three ships. He left port on August 3, 1492, aboard the *Santa Maria*. The *Nina* and the *Pinta* were sailing close by. Columbus had charted a course to the southwest, avoiding the stormy seas of the North Atlantic.

On September 6, Columbus sailed west from the Canary Islands (see map, pages 32-33). He did not expect the voyage to

be a long one. Columbus had based his calculations on the map of a Florentine man named Toscanelli. This map showed the distance between Asia and Europe to be about 6,500 miles (the actual distance is 10,600 miles). What neither Columbus nor Toscanelli knew was that America lay in between.

As the days dragged on, the sailors began to grumble. It was not a comfortable journey. The food was always the same: heavily salted meat, hard biscuits, and beans. The drink was always red wine — until it gave out. Then the crew had only stale water. The captain alone had a cabin and a bunk. Everyone else just slept wherever a spot was available.

The ships passed through plenty of seaweed, but no one sighted land. The sailors almost mutinied after sailing for a month into the unknown. Columbus himself was encouraged by the birds flying overhead. These birds slept on land. He reasoned that they could fly only so far out to sea in the course of a day.

On October 9, branches with green leaves were seen floating in the water. The green leaves suggested that the branches had been recently torn from a tree. The shore must be near. Finally land was sighted at night by a lookout, Rodrigo de Triana, on October 12, 1492. This was an island in the Bahamas most recently identified as Samana Cay. Columbus called it San Salvador.

Columbus continued on through the Caribbean, stopping at Hispaniola and other islands (see map, pages 32-33). On his way

Columbus left Spain aboard the **Santa Maria** *on August 3, 1492. When he landed safely in the Bahamas on October 12, he believed he was only a few miles off the eastern coast of China.*

home his ship was almost wrecked in a storm. He was lucky to live through it and return to Spain to report his discovery.

This first voyage made Columbus a hero, an admiral, and a powerful man. He enjoyed his position for a while before making plans for a second voyage in 1497. On this second trip he sailed through the Caribbean, visiting Cuba, Jamaica, and Puerto Rico. But Columbus had a problem. He had not found China or Japan. He had only found lots of islands and plenty of mosquitoes.

He returned to Spain without much good to say. Ferdinand and Isabella did not give up on him yet, though. They sent him back on a third voyage in 1498. On this trip he discovered more islands and the coast of South America. But Columbus didn't know it was the coast of a new continent. In fact, he had trouble fitting it into his map. He still believed he was somewhere near China.

Columbus later stopped at the Spanish colony he had helped establish on Hispaniola. The officials there were corrupt, and many people were sick. Columbus tried to govern the Spaniards himself, but some of them rebelled against him. Columbus hanged the rebels, but was then arrested by a newly arrived representative of the king. He was returned to Spain in chains. Ferdinand and Isabella ordered him freed at once, saying his arrest had been a mistake.

By now Columbus was getting old and tired. He also suffered from arthritis. He still hoped, though, to find proof that he had discovered Asia. In 1502 he got his last chance. He set sail with four ships and 135 men. They arrived in the Caribbean safely, but storms followed them everywhere after that. Columbus searched high and low for India, China, or Japan. All he found was Central America and more islands. His battered ships became so damaged that he had to abandon them in Jamaica. Columbus spent the next year there waiting to be rescued. A ship finally appeared, and he was taken home to Spain.

Although Columbus achieved lasting fame, he died an unhappy man. A master seaman, he was also very stubborn. Until his death in 1506 he continued to claim that he had reached the Indies of Asia. By that time few other people agreed with him.

One man who had shared Columbus' hope for sailing west to the Orient was John Cabot of Bristol, England. He had been born Giovanni Caboto in Genoa sometime around 1450. He came to England in 1493 after living in Venice for at least fifteen years. He had traveled much in the Middle East. One place he had visited was the Arabian city of Mecca, where spices and other goods arrived from Asia (see map, page 46).

This sight may have spurred him on to find an Atlantic route to China. So why did he go to Bristol? For one thing, Bristol was in the north. Like Columbus, Cabot knew the world was round. He reasoned that a trip westward in the north would be shorter than one closer to the equator. (Unlike Columbus he didn't worry about stormy seas.) For another thing, Bristol fishermen knew a lot about western waters. Bristol was a bustling city, known for exporting cloth, importing wine, and, most especially, for catching fish. Competition from foreign boats had pushed Bristol fishermen farther and farther west. By 1485

Bristol fishermen were probably fishing in the waters off the Newfoundland coast.

Cabot approached King Henry VII of England for royal approval of his proposed voyage. Henry was happy to sponsor him as long as he didn't have to spend any money. Fortunately the merchants of Bristol were paying for the trip.

Cabot set out with a crew of eighteen. The North Atlantic crossing was uneventful and land was sighted in June 1497. So here was Asia, thought Cabot. Actually it was Newfoundland (see map, pages 32-33). In fact, Cabot was not far from the place where Leif Ericson had built his house.

Cabot was a cautious man. He did not go ashore right away. He followed the coast for three hundred leagues (about nine hundred miles) before he landed. He saw no native Americans, but he did find some hunting snares, a needle for making nets, and some trees that had been cut down. He assumed from these signs that people must be nearby. He did not go looking for them, though. He simply returned to England.

Henry VII was very happy with Cabot's report. Cabot proposed a second voyage, and Henry was delighted to help. This time he gave Cabot ships, money, and even prisoners from the jails to be his crewmen.

The next year Cabot sailed west again. Still believing he had reached Asia, he intended to follow the coast south until he reached the Spice Islands (now known as the Moluccas). But somewhere on the way disaster struck. Nobody knows what

John Cabot, born Giovanni Caboto in Genoa, Italy, moved to Bristol, England in 1493. Four years later, in 1497, he sailed west from Bristol in hopes of discovering a sea route to Asia.

happened, but John Cabot and his ships were never heard from again.

Columbus and Cabot were the last true discoverers of America; the last to journey across the ocean without any proper idea of what they would find on the other side. It was another explorer, Amerigo Vespucci, who recognized the new lands for what they actually were.

Vespucci made three trips to America, the first in 1499. (He claimed to have discovered South America on an earlier trip in 1497, but he probably made this up.) His detailed description of his experiences were circulated widely in Europe. When a new map of the world was being drawn up to include the discovered continents between Europe and Asia, the mapmaker put the name "America" across Brazil. (He believed Vespucci's story about discovering South America in 1497, a year before Columbus.) Clearly, the name caught on.

EPILOGUE

So who really discovered America? Well, the Asian nomads discovered it by crossing the land bridge from Asia to Alaska. They settled northwest North America perhaps 40,000 years ago. Their descendants moved south and east, eventually discovering South America as well. Lost ships from China and India probably reached the west coast around 2,000 years ago, though exactly when and how remains unknown. The Polynesians did not depend on sails. They paddled thousands of miles across the Pacific by canoe. They came ashore at least several generations before any Europeans did. We don't know if they met anyone once they got here. But we do know they took the sweet potato home as a souvenir of their visit.

Atlantic crossings may have started with the Phoenicians being swept to Brazil by a storm. This probably didn't happen before the sixth century B.C. Bjarni Herjulfson accidentally bumped into northeast Canada 1,600 years later, prompting several Viking expeditions starting with Leif Ericson's. The Spanish under Columbus and the

English under Cabot completed the initial discovery of America at the end of the 1400's.

They were different people from different times, but they all shared one thing in common—none of them were looking for America when they found it. For some, like the first Asian nomads, who found a land full of wild game, the discovery was good luck. For others, like Cabot, who disappeared on his second voyage, it wasn't lucky at all. But lucky or not, the discoveries opened a new world. And the discoverers themselves set the course of American history. Their achievements continue to affect our lives even today.

INDEX

Italicized page numbers refer to illustrations